COVENANT

His Word. His Bond. His Son.

ESTHER HAYNES

WESTBOW
PRESS®
A DIVISION OF THOMAS NELSON
& ZONDERVAN

Scripture taken from the King James Version of the Bible.

WestBow Press books may be ordered through booksellers or by contacting:

WestBow Press
A Division of Thomas Nelson & Zondervan
1663 Liberty Drive
Bloomington, IN 47403
www.westbowpress.com
1 (866) 928-1240

ISBN: 978-1-5127-6874-9 (sc)
ISBN: 978-1-5127-6875-6 (e)

Library of Congress Control Number: 2016920749

Print information available on the last page.

WestBow Press rev. date: 01/23/2017

*To the children that God has blessed my husband
and me with—Richie, Gailie, and Dawnie—
and their "anointed, appointed" spouses*

*To the three grandchildren that God has blessed
us with—Alicia, Sydney, and Mikey*

*If I leave nothing in this world, I leave them and the
world as a better place because they are in it.*

CONTENTS

Foreword..ix
Acknowledgments...xi
Introduction...xiii

Chapter 1—God Is Great.................................... 1
Chapter 2—A Covenant in Blood........................11
Chapter 3—The Garden > The Cross > The Crown......16
Chapter 4—Search and Rescue 47
Chapter 5—An Enduring Legacy........................ 53

Epilogue.. 61
Bibliography.. 63

FOREWORD

THE OLD SAYING, "STILL waters run deep," has never been truer. Having known Sis Haynes for over fifteen years, I have come to know her as a woman of distinct faith and patience. As I read this text, it was a new revelation of the intense fire in her bosom and divinely inspired knowledge in her soul. Within these pages, you will find an opus to God's covenant. This well-crafted modern epistle surveys the central tenets of our faith, weaving a passionate tapestry. Through its passages, the reader will gain a richer understanding of God's redemptive plan, shared as only she can.

Sis Haynes brings a keen insight to scripture. She skillfully sifts through the biblical text, gleaning the most pertinent scriptures to illustrate God's redemptive plan for the church. Whether you are a new convert or seasoned theologian, this text will offer you a wealth of new insight as she shares scripture from a new perspective.

Thank you, Sister Haynes, for opening up the Bible in a new way.

Reverend Marlon P. Williams,
Pastor of Crystal Church

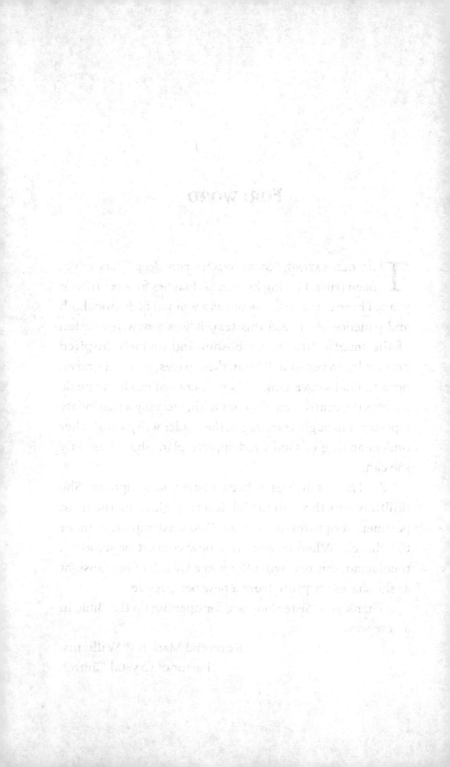

ACKNOWLEDGMENTS

I F THIS BOOK INSPIRES anyone other than myself, please know that the Holy Spirit inspired it. I only did the penmanship. My family is always a constant source of inspiration for me and every day makes my life worthwhile. My husband's encouragement and assistance was invaluable and very much appreciated.

My pastor, whose exuberance in ministering the Word, challenges us to give more than lip service to the Word and the work. My former pastor who laid a foundation in God's Word that is solid as the rock.

Finally, many thanks to all those who deposited into my spirit all my life long and a brilliant but humble young man who taught the other nine fingers to navigate the keyboard and the world of the computer.

INTRODUCTION

WE LIVE IN AN increasingly secular society that grows bolder in its defiance of God and His standards and demands. The de facto leader of this rebellion against God primarily and all the righteous limits He imposes to protect humanity is himself the enemy they fear God to be. He has blinded their eyes and led them away from the path that reveals God as a friend indeed and much more than that.

The deception persists and only grows more elaborate, and the consequences are graver. The only way out of the morass of this decadence is the way rejected and despised. Thankfully, it is the way that will triumph in the end, but not before the worst is yet to come.

It is urgent. Our duty is to be the voice crying, telling the story of redemption and life for whosoever will. So many broken lives, defeated by the world's empty promises, need to hear the promises of God that He covenanted by His own blood, His very own Son, the sacrifice.

Oh, how truly healing and restoring His love is! Peace for the turmoil in the soul. Eternally!

CHAPTER 1

GOD IS GREAT

T HE BOOK OF GENESIS outlines the odyssey of humankind's origin and downfall, along with the Creator's initiative to reset the course for righteousness on the earth. The word *genesis* means the beginning or coming into being of something. The canonical Bible begins with the book of Genesis, as does the Jewish Torah. Genesis opens with, "In the beginning God ..." (Gen. 1:1). The writer of the New Testament book of Hebrews tells us, "He that cometh to God must believe that He is ..." (Heb. 11:6). However, we are not left to believe in a vacuum. There is a preponderance of evidence both in scripture and in nature for the existence of God and His presence in the affairs of humankind.

God Speaks Clearly of Himself in His Word

- "For thus saith the Lord who created the heavens, God Himself who formed the earth and made it; He established it, He created it not in vain, He formed it to be inhabited. I am the Lord and there is none else" (Isa. 45:18).

- "I have made the earth, and created man upon it; I, even my hands have stretched out the heavens, and all their hosts have I commanded" (Isa. 45:12).
- "Thus saith the Lord, the King of Israel and his Redeemer, the Lord of Hosts, I am the first and I am the last, and beside me there is no God" (Isa. 44:6).

The Declaration Is Both Clear and Emphatic

There is no ambiguity. There is one God and no others! God faces off with the puny gods of humanity's making as well as with the forces on the earth that challenge His supreme authority and power. No defense is mounted against His claim to sovereignty over all the earth, the heavens, and everything that exists or ever existed. All the evidence supports God's declaration that He is the Creator. "Behold, ye are nothing and your work of naught; an abomination is he who chooses you" (Isa. 41:24).

God roundly debunks false gods and claims and those who are duped by them. He declared to the patriarch Abraham, "I am the Almighty God" (Gen. 17:1). And Jeremiah 32:27 says, "Behold, I am the Lord, the God of all flesh. Is anything too hard for me?" 1 Chronicles 29:11,12 KJV says,

> Thine, O Lord, is the greatness, and the power, and the glory, and the victory, and the majesty; for all that is in the heaven and in the earth is thine. Thine

is the Kingdom, O Lord, and thou art exalted as head above all; both riches and honor come of thee, and thou reignest over all; and in thine Hand is power and weight; and in thine hand it is to make great, and to give strength to all.

God Confirmed His Omnipotence

God is Lord over all, and He rules in the affairs of humanity, both kingdoms and powers. "Blessed be the name of God forever and ever, for wisdom and might are His, and He changed the times and the seasons; He removeth kings and setteth kings up; He giveth wisdom unto the wise, and knowledge to those who know understanding" (Dan. 2:21). And Daniel 5:21 says, "Till he [Nebuchadnezzar] knew that the Highest God ruled in the kingdom of men, and that He appointed over it whomsoever He will."

God is present in humanity's affairs. He isn't an absentee deity with a hands-off approach to the day-to-day, down-to-earth life issues. He is our Father with a heart like a mother. His heart senses a need that cannot be put into words and is sensitive to our frailties and failures. His heart actively seeks to give, bless, and equip us with the tools we need to "live and move and have our being." He is our partner, and He knows all things in real time. "For His eyes are upon the ways of man, and He seeth all his goings" (Job 34:21).

God Expressed His Omniscience

The omniscience of the Godhead was reflected in Jesus during His ministry while He was here on earth. "But Jesus did not commit Himself unto them, because He knew all men, and needed not that any should testify of man; for He knew what was in man" (John 2:24–25).

Jesus oftentimes responded to the thoughts of those around Him, even though they did not voice those thoughts. "Now when the Pharisee who had bidden Him saw it, he spoke within himself … And Jesus answering him said" (Luke 7:39–40).Omniscience is a divine attribute manifested by Jesus the Christ on more than one occasion during His earthly ministry.

The awesome presence of God is everywhere in His vast universe. "Whither shall I go from thy Spirit? Or whither shall I flee from thy Presence? If I ascend up into heaven, thou art there; if I take the wings of the morning and dwell in the uttermost parts of the sea, even there shall thy hand lead me, and thy right hand shall hold me" (Ps. 139:7–10).

"The eyes of the Lord are in every place, beholding the good and the evil" (Prov. 15:3).

God Confirms His Omnipresence

He is everywhere present at once. He commands the forces of nature: elements and animals alike. "They all shall sweetly obey my will" (#102, *Favorite Hymns of Praise*).

- "Knowest thou the time when the wild goats of the rock bring forth? Or canst thou mark when the hinds do calve?" (Job 39:1).
- "Will the wild ox be willing to serve thee?" (Job 39:9).

- "Doth the eagle mount up at thy command?" (Job 39:27).
- "Canst thou draw out Leviathan? Will he make supplications unto thee? Will he make a covenant with thee?" (Job 41:1, 3, 4).

The animal kingdom instinctively knows and responds to God's plan for its existence and survival in the predatory world in which it exists. Perhaps nowhere else are we able to see the animal kingdom display that instinctive bent to survival than in places like the African savannah in the Serengeti (for example, Serengeti National Park, Tanzania, Africa, 1951. Google/Wikipedia free encyclopedia). Multiple television features and documentaries give us front-row seats.

As various dramas play out before us, the precision of the handiwork of God's creation awes us. "These all wait upon thee, that thou mayest give to them their food in due season. That which thou givest them they gather; thou openest thine hand, they are filled with good" (Ps. 104:27–28).

The book of Daniel gives the account of Daniel's encounter with the lions when he was thrown into their den. He did not have to lay a violent hand on the lions to escape from their claws, teeth, and overwhelming strength. Contrary to their natural inclination, the lions became docile before him. Was their allegiance to Daniel? Were they in awe or in dread of Daniel, an intruder into their territory and a natural enemy? I think not. They recognized the voice of He who called them into being, their Creator.

The Elements Are Subject to Their Creator

Numerous accounts in scripture clearly show the elements in nature responding to their Creator. In the first place, as alluded to previously, God spoke them into being. He parted the Red Sea for Moses. He made the sun stand still and parted the Jordan River for Joshua, Moses's successor. And that's just to name a few.

- "He directed ... His lightening unto the end of the earth. He thundereth with the voice of His excellency" (Job 37:3).
- "For He maketh small drops of water; they pour down rain according to their vapor, which clouds do drop and distill upon man abundantly" (Job 36:27–28).
- "Or who shut up the sea with doors ... and said, thus far shalt thou come, but no further; and here shall thy proud waves be stayed?" (Job 38:8-11).
- "Then He arose, and rebuked the winds and the sea; and there was a great calm" (Matt. 8:26).

God is always in charge of everything. And everything and everyone are always under the subjection of His mighty power and sovereign will. However, we can always take comfort in the knowledge that God's thoughts toward us are "thoughts of peace, and not to evil, to give you an expected end" (Jer. 29:11). This is the God who, in His grace and mercy, made the decision by Himself to enter into a covenant with His fallen world.

Covenant: A Binding Agreement

Covenants in biblical times were often sealed in blood by severing an animal, with the implication that the party who breaks the covenant would suffer the same fate. The new covenant is considered a bond in blood sovereignly administered by God. A covenant in blood is unbreakable for the life of the parties. The inference is that each party brings something worthy of the transaction to the table.

Humankind had only its sin, and God had all the worthy resources. Only humans stood to gain from a covenant with God. On the other hand, God would gain His fallen creation at great cost to Himself. God must become a man and die a cruel death for all humankind. He must pay the debt we owed to Him so He could pardon us from that debt and death, our earning from sin.

His pursuit of us is relentless. His love for us is boundless. He will not rest while we are in sin. He will seek us and save us if we choose to respond, accept, and receive Him. He gave all that ever needed to be given. He provided all that was needed for the redemption of His children. He has continually sought after us, His children, even when we refuse His overtures for reconciliation. How humbling!

In spite of it all, God made a covenant with humanity. He went to the limits of sacrifice to make it happen for our sakes. He lowered Himself to the bar of justice and placed Himself under scrutiny by His own creation. He went toe to toe with the enemy of humanity's soul because He would not leave us in captivity. When, by default, we came under the dominion of the adversary of God Himself and all of creation, God's heart was moved with compassion for our condition and impending doom.

Imagine for a moment, the state that those two distraught and frightened human beings were in after the craftiness of the devil and their own lust had deceived them (James 1:14). They had just handed over all that God entrusted to them and, along with themselves, sold every succeeding human being to ever grace Planet Earth into slavery to sin and the very archenemy of God. And imagine for a moment, God, as was His custom, coming into the garden and surveying the aftermath of what was literally the greatest misfortune of all time.

What will He say? What will He do? How will He react? It's just a few of the questions that just possibly might have been on the mind of those two desperate, sad, utterly confused, and bewildered souls. God, a father with a heart like a mother, did not go off on a tirade and unleash what would have been justified wrath into this incredibly heartrending scene. God instead administered His love, the great love with which He loved us, even all of us yet unborn.

He immediately went to work reversing the curse. He immediately took on Satan on behalf of His defeated children, and He set His plan of redemption in motion, which was conceived before the foundation of the world and activated on day one of the crisis. There was no time to waste prolonging the agony, scoring points, and playing the blame game. There was a monumental task at hand, and the time to get started was now. God exercised His sovereign authority and took charge of the situation, and He vowed to those trembling souls that He would redeem and restore them to their lost estate.

A Covenant Was Made

"God is not a man that He should lie" (Num. 23:19). "He knoweth our frame" (Ps. 103:14). God our Father is under no illusion about our frailties, shortcomings, and weaknesses. He works tirelessly, mercifully, and graciously with us—all our life long—to renew us by teaching us through His Word and His servants. He doesn't leave us floundering in our mishaps without a path out. Hebrews 13:5 says, "I will never leave thee nor forsake thee."

Could it be that Adam and Eve were the first ones to hear that solemn promise? I am just thinking. Hallelujah! From then on, God made covenants with humble, fallen human beings and the whole world. His Word is above reproach and always proven good. An entire universe lends its support to the absolute truth of God's Word. Archeological finds have unearthed long-lost evidence to corroborate so much of what the Word of God says and nothing to disprove it. But that notwithstanding, He meets us at our level and is ever doing the work in us to bring us up to His level. He saw fit to make covenant with humankind so He is held accountable for His Word of promise. We are legally entitled to say to the great, the Most High God, "You have a covenant with us, and we expect you would do what you say you would. Therefore we believe you."

Genesis 3:15 says, "Her seed; He shall bruise thy head and thou shalt bruise His heel." Hope sprang up in the hearts of Adam and Eve, in the midst of their grief, sorrow, and turmoil. All was not lost for all time. God will turn things around!

On any given day, we could see a most beautiful visual

of another covenant God made with humankind. On a rainy day, it is a welcome sight to see an array of beautiful colors in the sky—colors that inspire many an artist's masterpiece or designer's dream collection. God created it to be a permanent reminder of His covenant with us.

Genesis 9:9, 13–16 says, "And I, behold I establish my covenant with you and with your seed after you … I do set my bow in the cloud, and it shall be for a token of a covenant between me and the earth … the waters shall no more become a flood to destroy all flesh and the bow shall be in the cloud."

In the thousands of years since that bow was placed in the sky and that covenant was put in the book, never has there been a flood to wipe out the whole earth. Who can tell the end from the beginning: man or God? God made a covenant, and it is so. God promised Abraham by covenant: a nation, a country, and a seed. And from the blessing of Abraham, it was to bless the whole world. Gal. 3:14 says, "That the blessing of Abraham might come on the Gentiles through Jesus Christ, that we might receive the promise of the Spirit through faith."

Have we received the promise? Has God's Word been true? Can we question His Integrity? Has God delivered or not? He absolutely has! Does anyone care to dispute that? Isaiah 41:28 says, "For I beheld and there was no man; even among them and there was no counselor that when I asked of them, could answer a word." And Psalm 119:89 says, "Forever O Lord, thy word is settled in heaven."

CHAPTER 2

A COVENANT IN BLOOD

"A COVENANT THAT IS SEALED in blood is a covenant forever." God formed a relationship with man that is based on a covenant. Man hates God's way, but "God so loved the world that He gave His Only Son (John 3:16). In His blood, Jesus satisfied all the prerequisites of establishing a blood covenant and was our ample representative in the cutting of the covenant of the New Testament.

With all we know about the binding, enduring aspect, and absolute aspect of the blood covenant, we can—in fact, it is imperative—believe God's Word, His promises. If man puts implicit faith in a blood covenant made among men, can we even dare to do less than put implicit faith in a blood covenant made by God with the very Son of God, His only begotten as the sacrificial Lamb, His the blood of the everlasting covenant?

"The most binding agreement in all of humanity, a blood covenant" is the eternal bond between God and His people, His children. He cannot go back on the Word of promise that has gone out of His mouth. No promise He has uttered can fail because that will undoubtedly bring scathing dishonor to His great name.

In light of this, how then should we react to His promises? How would we justify our failure to grasp with our might—our mind, heart, soul, and strength—all the benefits that God (Father, Son, and Holy Spirit) has provided for us in this gold standard of binding agreements, "the blood covenant—from which there is no retreat." How could we?

Sadly, much too easily. Even with a blood covenant initiated and executed by God Himself, "the new covenant in His blood," mankind opts for godless ideologies and philosophies, failed human promises and agreements, deals and treaties—self and Satan. Man rejects the love of God and the Word of God. Yet God "daily loadeth us up with benefits" (Ps.68:19), not the least of which is the breath of life essential to our existence and which very existence we would rather use to denigrate and malign and dismiss Him as a figment of man's imagination. In fact, God is ridiculed, mocked, and relegated to the realm of the ignorant and feebleminded. But God confirms His supreme authority and His unquestionable status as the one true and living God, the Creator.

On day five of creation, "God said …" and the waters and the air was teeming with life—newly created life. On the sixth day of creation "God said …" and the earth was filled with "cattle" and "creeping things" and "beasts of the earth." And finally God created His crowning achievement in creation—He made man in His own image after His likeness: "male and female created He them" (Gen. 1:27).

By this time, the creation of the elements and

vegetation—vital to the survival of the sixth-day newcomers—had been put in place and was up and running according to plan. And so it has been ever since, notwithstanding man's flagrant disregard for God's instructions.

Genesis 2:1, 3 says, "Thus the heavens and the earth were finished and all the hosts of them. And God blessed the seventh day and sanctified it, because that in it He rested from all His work which God created and made."

And Acts 17:24, 25 says, "God who made the world and all things in it, seeing that He is Lord of Heaven and earth, dwelled not in temples made with hands, nor is worshipped with men's hands as though He needs anything, seeing He giveth to all life and breath and all things."

God confirmed Himself the Creator. He is maker, innovator if you will, of all that is seen and unseen. Man did not make up God; God made man. And God made us His covenant partners, "friends of God."

"A blood covenant between two parties: be it two individuals, or two clans or maybe two tribes, could involve either cutting the palms or cutting the wrists from whence the blood could be mingled either by shaking hands or joining at the wrists; or the blood of both parties could be allowed to fall into a single vessel of wine and both parties then partake of the common cup." (Google/online, The Covenant Kingdom by Rob Board).

The procedure was no doubt a bloody event. When it involved slaying of animals, it again would have been a very bloody exercise. In God's covenant with Abraham, it was awash with blood. There was the blood of the slain animals. There was also "the blood that accompanied the circumcision of every male." In the covenant with Moses on behalf of the children of Israel, there was an ever-present flow of blood. It was a bloody scene made necessary because of man's ever-present sin and sinful nature.

To cut the new covenant, however, must have required a bloodbath, an atonement that is efficacious enough to wash away all sin from every soul who ever lived—past, present, and future. The new and everlasting covenant in the blood of the Son of God Himself, that alone would satisfy all the requirements of a just and holy God in order to grant clemency to an evil and sinful world; to pay the price of redemption and salvation; to bring reconciliation with the Holy God; and to restore the lost estate and position in creation. A bloodbath indeed!

Isaiah 52:14 says, "As many were astounded at thee— His visage was so marred more than any man and His form, more than the sons of men." And Matthew 27:29a, 30 states, "And when they had plaited a crown of thorns, they put it upon his head … And they spat upon Him, and took the reed and smote him on the head." John 19:1 says, "Then Pilate therefore took Jesus and scourged Him."

Scourge means "whip; lash; to punish severely." (Merriam-Webster's Pocket Dictionary)

John 19:17 says, "And He bearing His cross, went forth unto a place called the place of the skull, which is called in the Hebrew—Golgotha, where they crucified Him." It was a vicious brutal beating followed by crucifixion (put to death on a cross). Our Lord had to endure this cruel humiliation that was usually reserved for the worst criminals.

Isaiah 53:12 says, "He was numbered with the transgressors." And Exodus 4:26 says, "So she let him

(Moses) go; then she said, a bloody husband thou art because of the circumcision."

Our Lord Jesus was mercilessly flogged. "He was wounded for our transgression, He was bruised for our iniquities ... and with His stripes we are healed." Crucified, He endured a shameful death for our sin. A new covenant sealed with the blood of the Lamb slain before the foundation of the world. An everlasting covenant cut with a veritable bloodbath. A bloody husband indeed was He to the bride of Christ. John 15:13 says, "Greater love hath no man than this that a man lay down his life for his friends."

Jesus Christ, our Savior and Lord, laid down His life for His church—His brethren by blood covenant, joint heirs with Him to all the Father has provided and prepared for His church—life abundantly and life eternal. He gave healing for our sicknesses and renewal day by day. He gave daily provision as He does for the birds of the air and the flowers of the field. He gave freedom from captivity of the enemy of our soul. Saved, we are safe from the powers of darkness and free from exclusion from the promises of the covenant. We are given blood-bought benefits for the child of God, whoever you are, whosoever will.

Ephesians 3:9, 11 says, "And to make all see what is the fellowship of the mystery which from the beginning of the ages has been hidden in God who created all things through Jesus Christ ... According to the eternal purposes which He accomplished in Christ Jesus our Lord."

As He hung on the cross, paying the awful sin debt for humankind with His life ebbing away, Jesus uttered one of His famous last words, "It is finished."

But where did it begin?

CHAPTER 3

THE GARDEN > THE
CROSS > THE CROWN

The Garden

WHEN SATAN ENTERED THE garden of Eden, he met Adam and Eve fresh off God's hand of creation. Not only did God form man, God breathed His life into man. And Satan challenged these perfectly created beings on that fateful day. And man fell in the first round. Satan did not have to come back time and again and wear them down. He conquered them in one round. Man fell and lost his estate, and Satan was in legal control. God has always been in absolute control, but in His nature of justice, fairness, and righteousness, God allowed Satan the victory on legal grounds. But Satan always knew he was at a disadvantage because his was a losing battle. Why? His fight was not with man, but with God—his maker, his master, his ultimate destroyer.

God engaged Satan as a monarch would engross an equal in a fair fight, "for the gain of man's soul or its loss."

God, who has absolute power, love, and justice, submitted Himself to legal scrutiny. God lowered Himself from the realm of His sovereign deity to the realm of humanity for His creation. He chose to make His case for the lordship of humankind and all of creation at the bar of justice.

Isaiah 41:21–23 says,

> Produce your cause, saith the Lord, bring forth your strong reasons, saith the King of Jacob. Let them bring them forth and show us what shall happen; let them show the former things what they are that we may consider them and know the latter end of them; or declare us things to come. Show the things that are to come hereafter, that we may know that ye are gods; yea do good or do evil that we may be dismayed and behold it together.

God prosecutes His case. He invites us to hold Him up to intense scrutiny. Bring your evidence that refutes His claims. Isaiah 40:14 says, "With whom took He counsel, and who instructed Him … and taught Him knowledge, and showed to Him the way of understanding."

God makes His case. Isaiah 43:26 says, "Put me in remembrance; let us plead together; declare thou that thou mayest be justified."

No challenge is mounted by any opposition against the Lord of all. Isaiah 44:6 says, "Thus saith the Lord, the King of Israel and his Redeemer, the Lord of hosts: I am the first and I am the last and beside me there is no god."

God is clear in His closing arguments, "I have made the earth and created man upon it; I even my hands, have stretched out the heavens and all their hosts have I commanded."

The jury is in! God renders the judgment. He alone is God, and there is no other. There is no competition. This is still—and always is—God's earth, His world, His universe. He is in charge here. God invites man to investigate and search out to "taste and see." Man ventures into the vastness of knowledge. Does God approve? Absolutely! Does God give man the ability, capability, intelligence, and even privilege of deciphering and defining the mysteries of the universe through the vehicle of science in all its various branches? Certainly! God allows it. But why? For the same reason He placed Himself at the bar of justice. Investigate, and get a personal experience, a revelation. You are encouraged to not take anyone's word for it. Check it out and see for yourself. The conclusion you come to will either exonerate or condemn you. The verdict is already read. God is already exonerated. Isaiah 45:22 says, "Look unto me, and be saved, all the ends of the earth; for I am God and there is none else."

Enter Jesus Christ, God the Son in the form of man, Daniel's Son of Man. God became man, Emmanuel, God with us. And in the form of man, He took on a rematch with Satan in the very same arena as the first match played out, Planet Earth. Satan knows he cannot go toe to toe with God. But he had already gone head to head with man and defeated him in one round. He must have felt his prospects were good. Jesus is God, but here He is on Satan's turf in the form of man. Satan may have felt that it might take more than one round to conquer this man, but maybe he felt he could break Him as man, if he kept the pressure on. As it turned out, the strategy that won him so many victories over so many humans so many times would not succeed with this man, the man Christ Jesus.

John 14:30 says, "The prince of this world cometh, and hath nothing in me." The prince of this world was never able to conquer Jesus. He was never able to cause Jesus to disobey His Father, do His own will, or carry out His own agenda. Never. Not once. Jesus was on a mission. He stayed on message. He moved steadfastly forward on God's agenda, always carrying forward God's eternal plan of salvation.

When God approached those two frightened, bewildered souls in the garden of Eden way back when, He came with a plan and purpose: grace and redemption. That plan was formulated before the foundation of the world. He knew that man was vulnerable. One-third of the angels that were in heaven, in God's continuous presence and jurisdiction, fell with Satan. Humankind met a similar fate. But God already had devised His plan. In His mercy and grace, He came to the rescue when Satan undoubtedly thought he surely had humankind for the taking. Satan could not envision that God would go to such great lengths of love and grace in order to redeem His fallen children, but God had a plan!

The Cross

He would pay the price Himself to restore fallen man to Himself. God's plan was woven all through the ages from the garden to the cross. He painstakingly, lovingly, and mysteriously steered His plan until finally the strategy of the enemy culminated with the plot to kill the Lord—the betrayal, the denial, and the decision. "Crucify Him!" Then there was the vicious, brutal beating and the humiliating, horrifying crucifixion.

As Jesus hung battered, bruised, and mortally wounded on the cross of Calvary, the plan of redemption, the new covenant in His blood, was now mission accomplished. Our Lord is victorious over the enemy. This, Satan could not imagine. He never saw it coming! Such love was beyond his scope of comprehension. Unwittingly, he created the environment for God's plan to be flawlessly executed.

1 Corinthians 2: 7–8 says, "But we speak the wisdom of God in a mystery, even the hidden wisdom which God ordained before the ages unto His glory; which none of the princes of this age knew; for had they known it, they would not have crucified the Lord of glory."

With Jesus came grace and truth. Grace is the cornerstone of the covenant; truth is the Word of God. His grace is the reason man has survived. His grace was ready and waiting at the fall of humankind. Had God's grace not intervened, humankind would have perished from off the earth. The earth could have perished from the universe. Creation would have been a failed experiment. But God! But for God's grace! Does God create and is not able to sustain? Rubbish! Does God speak and is not able to perform? Ridiculous! Does God promise and is not able to deliver. Heresy!

God creates; God sustains. God delivers; God maintains for all eternity. He knows the end from the beginning. He knew at creation all that would transpire through all of earth's history. He created all things to be a resounding success. Earth succeeds; humankind succeeds. The planet survives through God's grace, His unmerited favor. How amazing!

Hebrews 10:19,20 KJV says, "Having therefore brethren, boldness to enter into the holiest by the blood of Jesus. By a new and living way, which He consecrated for us, through the veil, that is to say His flesh." Jesus gave Himself to be the sacrificial lamb, and in His blood, God made the new covenant with and on behalf of His created fallen beings. Under the old covenants, God stood with our fallen parents in the garden, with an obscure ship builder named Noah and an idol worshipper named Abram, and He continued down that lineage with the deceitful grandson Jacob. He brought Moses out of his hideout in the desert and raised him to prominence. He anointed a shepherd boy to be king over His people and forefather of the King of Kings, not to mention a harlot and a young pagan woman in the lineup.

And the list goes on, even down to the least among us. In fact, during His sojourn here on earth, Jesus's command center was amidst the least. His selective service was from the least, and it was the least among us that He tirelessly defended, commended, and deployed. In the new covenant, God became man and "dwelt amongst us." That man is the central figure of the covenant. "He represents God on the one hand and advocates for man on the other hand." He was the "perfect atonement offered for the forgiveness of sins."

As a king, He could have made covenant with the royal house. As a priest, He could have made covenant with the priestly order. But He made covenant as Savior, and whosoever will may come from the least to the greatest and vice versa. With the transaction completed, the covenant was enacted. Jesus now calls us to become partakers of the fellowship of covenant brethren, the church of the Lord Jesus Christ.

Matthew 11:28–30 says, "Come unto me all ye that labor and are heavy laden and I will give you rest; take my yoke upon you and learn of me, for I am meek and lowly in heart and ye shall find rest unto your souls; for my yoke is easy and my burden is light."

He came so we might have a more abundant life and exemplify His code of ethics in our daily living and relating to others. We are the visible body of Christ on the earth. Do people see Jesus walking on earth today in the flesh? Yes, they do. They see me, and they see you. The question is: what do they see? What they see in you and me may determine how they perceive Jesus. Will it draw them to Him as a magnet, or will it repel them like a negatively charged ion? We are Jesus's ambassadors to lost humanity. We, the church, must show and tell the world that God is love and He loves them. He paid an exorbitant price for their redemption, deliverance, and salvation.

He has thrown open wide His door, and He stands at our door knocking, inviting and pleading even. So grave is the consequence of sin; so free is the remedy. The church of the Lord Jesus Christ is a force for the greatest good on the most fronts for the world. It is Christlike to move with compassion to alleviate suffering and to bring wholeness into lives that are in need. God's Word requires us to do so. This was the hallmark of Jesus's ministry on earth.

Luke 13:16 says, "And ought not this woman, being a daughter of Abraham, whom Satan hath bound, lo these eighteen years, be loosed from this bond on the Sabbath

Day." Jesus was incensed at the stoniness of the heart on display that day in the synagogue. A sting accompanies the phrase "ought not." That mind-set and attitude that ignores the plight of a fellow human being to promote an idle ideology brings grief to the heart of God. The bond of love gave rise to the tremendous covenant of grace (and mercy) that we live under as children of God. The reality of what God has done for us, for our redemption, is both mind-blowing and mind-boggling. Such love has only one origin, God Himself. God is love!

God's love imparted to us propels us to be sowers in others' lives into their life situations: crises, emergencies, and devastations in all its forms. Why do ordinary people leave everything behind, risking everything to go to hostile places like crack houses, brothels, and dark, dangerous streets to rescue the perishing? They go because Jesus is there and He beckons. He knows the lost and desperate souls. They go because He loves them anyhow. He died to atone for them too. So He says "go," even unto the ends of the earth. He goes with you, even unto the ends of the earth! Mark 16:15 says, "And He said unto them, Go ye into all the world, and preach the gospel to every creature."

The message of the gospel—redeeming man—is meant for every creature to hear. Salvation is not a prize or an award. It is a gift from God to a lost and dying world. And the Bible tells us that such was some of us. Too often we allow our salvation to become a kind of trophy acknowledging our goodness and faithfulness, our devout godliness and extreme spirituality.

Really our salvation speaks of God's extreme love. The goal of our hearts then must be for others to have a go at Jesus and salvation. It's all about all the world with no exceptions, that is, have brethren among every people. What a noble mission! The Christ of Calvary stretched forth His arms to embrace everyone. His heart broke and bled for humankind everywhere. There is always room at the cross, be it for one or thousands. Everyone and anyone is too valuable to lose in God's eyes.

Isaiah 53:6 says, "All we like sheep have gone astray; we have turned everyone to his own way, and the Lord hath laid on Him the iniquity of us all." And Matthew 24:14 reads, "And this gospel shall be preached in all the world for a witness unto all nations; and then shall the end come."

But not before they've all had a chance to hear and accept that all may come. He wants them all to come, but He knows they won't all come, and He knows only too well the consequences of refusing the invitation. He gives the opportunity. He gives the moment. He cannot give the order. He gave humankind the freedom to choose, and He allows man's free will to trump His sovereign power and authority. Man is a free moral agent.

Unfortunately the choices man is apt to make and the road he is inclined to walk leads to so many perils. God lays out His way and His will, but it is met with utter disregard. We have gone from polite refusal to what is now wanton rebellion against God and anything that even remotely pertains to God. The world has drifted so far away from the foundation of the Bible that God is considered little more than a necessary nuisance.

The church of Jesus Christ must stand in stark contrast to the hostility and divisiveness that pervades the world around it. As the recipients of the blessings of the new covenant, we the church must be cognizant of the benefits and power that our heavenly Father makes available to us so we could live for Him and carry out our God-given tasks. It is important that we do not neglect to "build up ourselves in our most holy faith" (Jude 20) or to "study to show ourselves approved" (2 Tim. 2:15).

The marvelous provisions bought for us at such a high cost—the unimaginable suffering of the Son of the Most High God—will avail us little if anything unless we know who we are, more importantly who He is to us and what His sacrifice not only delivered us from but delivered to us. Christ's sacrifice on Calvary delivered us from eternal damnation and empowered us to live an overcoming life here and now.

- Saved from sin—everlasting death and hell
- Reconciliation to God
- Healing—and health—by His stripes
- Protection from the wiles of the devil
- Indwelling Holy Spirit—"the spirit of wisdom and understanding..." (Isa. 11:2)
- Eternal life and life more abundant

An impressive trove indeed

Therein is the potential for the life of victory in a world of defeat. The church must always be on the cutting edge of service, redemption, and reconciliation. The church of Jesus Christ is not to be trifled with, neither by the saints nor the sinners. The power of the Almighty God is resident within our ranks, and the world would do well to take note that the church is a force to be reckoned with. "The gates of hell shall not prevail against it" (Matt. 16:18).

It is the Word!

His bond, the Word; the Spirit; the Blood, binds us in heart and spirit to our Heavenly Father, to our Lord Jesus and to each other as believers in Christ. A common bond that inspires our worship to one God and Father and evokes praises to one Savior, Jesus Christ the Lord.

Ephesians 1:13–14 says, "In whom ye also trusted, after ye heard the word of truth, the gospel of your salvation; in whom also after ye believed, ye were sealed with that Holy Spirit of promise, who is the earnest of our inheritance until the redemption of the purchased possession, unto the praise of His glory."

"In covenant, you are no longer concerned only with yourself. Your concern must now include your covenant brother." In the church of Jesus Christ, the Holy Spirit makes this bond so real to the children of God. The Holy Scriptures is replete with admonitions to be concerned with the welfare of others. The early church exemplified a model of charitable concern for each other that truly must challenge the children of God everywhere. The love of God holds fast that bond that joins our hearts together across the spectrums of race and nationality, color, and status.

1 John 2:10 says, "He that loveth his brother abideth in the light and there is no occasion of stumbling in him." And 1 John 3:16 reads, "By this perceive we the love of God, because He laid down His life for us; and we ought to lay down our lives for the brethren."

God has woven the Holy Spirit into the fabric of the church of Jesus Christ, and no matter how far flung we are from each other, the common bond of the deep, abiding presence of God's Spirit joins our hearts. In the words of the old standard sung by saints of yesteryear, "There is a place where spirits blend; where friend holds fellowship with friend. Though sundered far by faith they meet; around one common mercy seat" (*Sankey's Sacred Songs and Solos*, #1171)

Our heavenly Father expects—in fact demands—we be as mindful of others as we are of ourselves. It cannot be just about us. "Oneness" is a recurring theme in the scriptures. It is conceived and birthed by sheer love, to put it simply. Love flowed from our Father as He stood amidst the thousand fragments of His newly formed creation, a scene the magnitude of which has been magnified and amplified with each passing age and eon. That love led to the cross "towering o're the wrecks of time." That love won my heart and yours and now bids us to "love one another." That love of God is revealed to us through His Son, channeled through us by His Holy Spirit and shared with a lost and dying world through His Word that inspires us to every good work. John 14:12 says, "Verily, verily, I say unto you, He that believeth on me, the works that I do shall he do also; and greater works than these shall he do."

God wires man for greatness. Many great works are done in His name and by His power. Many signs and wonders are wrought by His Holy Spirit through His ministering servants. Man's imagination, inventiveness, and creativity are all a legacy from the Creator Himself. However, with the passage of time, God has been stripped from prominence in the secular sphere of humankind's intellectual prowess. Man credits himself brazenly and unapologetically for the great achievements and the astonishing advancements across the intellectual spectrum. No glory is given to God even though it is He who deserves it all. Still God created man with enormous capacity and allows him autonomy. But none of man's achievements would be possible without God. All of it is possible without man.

Man overestimates his own importance and underestimates his own irrelevance. Should man disappear from the world, the earth would certainly become dramatically different, but it would continue to exist even if man does not. The reverse is not true. Nevertheless man is deceived into believing that he is in charge of his own destiny and he can chart his own course completely independent of God, on whom his next breath and beat of his heart entirely depends. Delusion!

Thankfully God is not a tyrant. He is a good God and a caring Father. It was His decision to make man as free moral beings. Despite the fact that the archenemy of God and man has pushed his strategy of diluting God out of man's thinking, he cannot defeat God's purpose any more than he could have stopped God's plan. God's Word has such enormous weight.

Psalm 138:2 says, "For thou hast magnified thy word above all thy name." God's Word is perfectly trustworthy. His prophets all bear Him witness that the Word of the Lord is truth, as prophecy is fulfilled time after time. Countless lives give testimony to the power of the Word of God by the dramatic transformation that takes place in the heart, the bold enthusiasm that consumes the spirit, and the refinement of the life made new in Christ by the Word and the Spirit. God's Word is His bond. God wired us for eternity. It is not a pipe dream we chase after. God has probably encoded it in our DNA! Genesis 3:22 says, "And the Lord God said: Behold, the man is become like one of us, to know good and evil; and now lest he put forth his hand and take of the tree of life and eat and live forever." God meant it so to be, but alas, it would have to wait. The evil deceiver put in his appearance to steal, kill, and destroy. Sin altered our course, outcome, and journey. But eternity remains in our core.

There are scenes in our life's journey that we wish we could hold on to, we revisit our whole life through, and we long to maintain as is, but time makes everything transient. And so with the passing of time, they are relegated to less and less prominence and eventually passes into the realm of precious memories. However, any trigger could rapidly transport us back to the scene with the same longing for it to go on forever.

It is not a daydream; it is our real reality. God created us for eternity, and time is unfortunately an intruder we have had to grow accustomed to. But God, in His grace and mercy, did not abandon us to our fate. He made a way to return us to eternity, even while He blesses us with abundant life here and now. Isn't it amazing?

God's grace and mercy knows no bounds. It transcends all boundaries and extends to friend and foe alike. He knows all things; He is an eyewitness. He cares for all; He surely aches for all. We humans feel such pain and devastation when tragedy in any form strikes. Within our relatively short life span, most, if not all of us, experience a fair share and some more than others do. The weeping, terrible heartache, and gut-wrenching, debilitating helplessness that these episodes bring into our lives, more often than not, cannot adequately be put into words. But I wonder how it must feel to God, who knows all things even before they ever occur and who has to look—maybe in horror—at the inevitable consequences of the choices we make that puts us in the line of fire. How could Adam and Eve have known that day that they set in motion a downward spiral that only the sacrifice of the Son of God could remedy. But God knew the hell—both literally and figuratively— that awaited humanity, the earth, and all of creation. He could look down through the ages and see each teardrop, every broken heart and spirit, the lost hope, and unfulfilled dreams and aspirations. He saw the wreckage of disease, habits, and lifestyles. He could view the corruption of morals and the loss of character and integrity. Standing in the garden of Eden on that fateful day, He could see it all. What was His heart like? The songwriter asks the question, "I wonder if God cries?" Did He? Wouldn't He?

1 John 4:10 says, "Herein is love, not that we loved God, but that He loved us, and sent His Son to be the propitiation for our sins."

"The love of God is greater far, than tongue or pen can ever tell." That's the amazing grace of God. I believe it infuriates Satan that God has fought so fiercely for His children. We are equipped for a fight. Satan is relentless in the war he wages on humankind as an affront to God, whom he knows he can never defeat. God does not leave our enemy with an unfair advantage over us. It is a battle we must fight, but with God's help, it is a bout we can ultimately win because Jesus already won the victory for us on the cross of Calvary. The great apostle Paul, nearing the end of his journey, left us these solemn words, "I have fought a good fight, I have finished my course, I have kept the faith" (2 Tim. 4:7).

"Fight the good fight." "Put on the whole armor of God." In so doing, thwart the game plan of the enemy and render him defeats instead of victory.

"Finish the course." "We are not of them who draw back unto perdition." Instead, we remember that we are covenant partners with the God of Creation; the God who stands alone from everlasting to everlasting; and the God who, with inexhaustible grace and mercy, condescended to our low estate to make an everlasting covenant with us in the blood of His Son, thus providing us access to the mighty weapons of our warfare and victory over the strongholds of the enemy. We can cross the finish line.

Hebrews 10:39 reads, "But of them that believe to the saving of the soul."

"Keep the faith". And why shouldn't we? The reward is worth the trial(s).

Romans 8:18 says, "For I reckon that the sufferings of this present time are not worthy to be compared with the glory which shall be revealed in us." His love compels us to become laborers together with Him to reclaim lost and dying humanity to His original intent; and to put down forever the dastardly works of the powers of darkness against the kingdom of light and life.

When God gave Adam dominion in the garden of Eden, He did not make him a figurehead. He gave him real authority over the earth. Thus when Satan duped Adam, Satan took real dominion over the earth. When Jesus told the disciples before His death, "Behold I give unto you power … over all the power of the enemy" (Luke 10:19), it was real power over the enemy and all his works that Jesus gave to them. And before His ascension, Jesus commanded His disciples to wait in the Upper Room for the promise of the Father, saying, "But ye shall receive power after that the Holy Ghost is come upon you" (Acts 1:8). They received real power and could not be stopped in their mission as they turned the world upside-down. And it is real power that we have over all the works of the enemy because we are partakers of the covenant.

It is so important for us, the children of God and followers of Jesus Christ—the blood-bought church of the Living God—to grasp the fact that God, our Father, is not derelict in His duties. All the provisions and the protection that is afforded in the covenant is available to us. But again, it is to no avail unless we truly come to terms, way down deep in our spirit, with the knowledge that God made a covenant with us, sealed in the blood of Jesus, and that a covenant is a binding agreement that honorable participants adhere to.

The good news is that God is not only an honorable participant, but He has our best interest at heart all the time. He has our backs! Also He placed the onus of fulfilling its demands on Himself. That's how amazing the grace of God truly is. The magnitude of the transaction that transpired at Calvary is incalculable in human terms. All we are called upon to do is believe.

Acts 16:31 says, "Believe on the Lord Jesus Christ and thou shalt be saved, and thy house." And Ephesians 2:8–9 reads, "For by grace are ye saved through faith; and that not of yourselves, it is the gift of God—not of works lest any man should boast."

Notice that God does not make a heavy-handed demand that you put up a required amount or degree of faith in order to have God respond to requests for His intervention and aid in our lives. He says, "Be it done unto you according to your faith." I do believe that "according to" references not an amount but rather the sincerity of the cry and resolve of the soul and spirit that God not only is very able but very willing to grant what the contrite heart is seeking.

Flippant, shallow, self-seeking requests cannot rise to this level of urgency and does not propel us into profound reverence and worship for His overarching love. This is when miracles are apt to happen. God's grace saturates the moment. Our faith soaks up the virtue and then increases and soars, and it sets us up for more and greater miracles. The faith cycle is on, unleashed against the works of the devil in our lives.

The gospel gives the account of Jesus in the boat with the disciples in the midst of a life-threatening storm. As Jesus miraculously stills the raging storm, the reaction of the disciples was "What manner of man is this?" (Matt. 8:27). In their second encounter with the same fate, Jesus ups the ante. He comes to them walking on the water! At the end of this event, however, their response is also kicked up a notch, "of a truth, thou art the Son of God" (Matt. 14:16).

A short time following this, Peter made his profound declaration, "Thou art the Christ [the Messiah on whom Israel was waiting for ages!], the Son of the Living God"

(Matt. 16:16) That's progress! Faith is less distant and more disciplined.

"Abraham believed God and He counted it to him for righteousness." Abraham took God at His word and followed through with obedience, and he became our towering figure of faith. God's covenant with Abraham—a blood covenant—gave him assurance that God meant what He said and He could absolutely be taken at His word. Abraham exercised his faith in God's Word when he was prepared to slay his son as a sacrifice to God at His bidding. It is just as reassuring to us. We are partners of the new and everlasting covenant that is sealed in the blood of the only begotten Son of God, a high value surety that adequately secures the children of God by covenant blessing to the Most Holy Father. We do well to be thus obedient to God's Word. Sacrifice will not substitute.

No detail is left to chance. There are no loopholes that the enemy can exploit. We come to God with our hearts. We "choose whom we will serve." God abides by our choice. (The devil, on the other hand, will usurp authority by default even if we don't outright choose him.) All our disqualifiers were nailed to the cross. The blood of Jesus has made us acceptable unto God.

Hebrews 9:14 says, "How much more shall the Blood of Christ, who through the Eternal Spirit offered Himself without spot to God, purge your conscience from dead works to serve the Living God." And 1 Peter 1:18 reads, "Forasmuch as ye know that ye were not redeemed with corruptible things like silver and gold ... But with the Precious Blood of Christ as of a lamb without spot and without blemish."

"The blood of Jesus" is not a cliché. It is not just words we repeat like a mantra. It calls to mind our covenant partnership with Father, Son, and Holy Ghost and all the hosts and resources of heaven! It is like calling up the army in a time of military invasion or an attack on the nation. As children of God who are saved by the blood of the Lamb and remain partners of the covenant, when we refer to the "blood of Jesus," we are in effect calling up the terms of the covenant to bring to bear on the circumstances at hand. The devil understands the strength of a covenant relationship. The devil knows that God is a responsible covenant partner, one who would not falter on His Word. God will watch over His Word to perform it. "The blood of Jesus" rallies the mighty host of heaven to the rescue, if only we comprehended the enormity of this heritage. But even with our limited scope, God responds to the full breadth of His provisions for our safety and well-being in the face of adversity. "The blood of Jesus" underscores the binding relationship God has fostered with us, His children.

We do well to be reminded that He cut a blood covenant on our behalf, from which He does not retreat, but from which all the forces of darkness must retreat when we exercise our right to enact it with confidence and faith in the Word of God.

We live in the shadow of the cross. At the cross of Jesus, our new life in Christ began. By the cleansing, atoning blood of Jesus, we revert from inherently evil to inherently good through Christ that lives in us; the Holy Ghost indwelling us; and the Word molding and shaping us. At the cross, the oasis of light was spawned to dispel the darkness encroaching on the earth. It took the precious blood of Jesus shed on the cross to combat the evil unleashed on the earth that day in Eden. Humankind was changed, no doubt at the level of his DNA, from inherently whole to inherently evil on that infamous day.

And we see in our time the evil hurtling to a crescendo. No amount of counteracting or contingencies would suffice to stop the decadence, the carnage, and the utter darkness that engulfs the world at large. All of man's measures has and always will be counterproductive. Evil is not an occurrence or an incident. It is a thread woven into the fabric of humanity, a sabotage of sorts, likened to the parable of Jesus.

Matthew 13:24, 25 says, "The Kingdom of heaven is likened unto a man who sowed good seed in his field; but while he slept, his enemy came and sowed tares among the wheat, and went his way." God is always awake and on duty, and He is never unawares. The devil's subversive act was foreseen, and God was already on offense. The outcome also was foreordained and predicted. The threat was neutralized.

It still takes only the blood, the name of Jesus, to stem the tide of evil in our midst. Only as man recognizes Jesus as the only and ultimate remedy will the human state improve or rather be transformed. Otherwise the fall continues to the bottomless pit. Thank God for Jesus. Thank God for the cross—death, resurrection, and ascension. God will restore us to a world where the real rule of law is truly observed: "love, joy, peace, longsuffering, gentleness, goodness, faith, meekness, self-control." And it's all because of the cross and the supreme sacrifice that paid our debt in full. With this as a backdrop, we will live eternally in the earth made new.

The Crown

The Lord urges us to "be thou faithful unto death, and I will give thee a crown of life" (Rev. 2:10). As Jesus was about to go to the cross, He comforted His disciples with these words that has been an encouragement to believers, the bride of Christ, for ages. John 14:1, 2, 27 reads, "Let not your hearts be troubled ... neither let it be afraid ... I go to prepare a place for you."

The tenderness of that moment is palpable. Confused and bewildered, these men who will eventually forge a movement that will transform the world and time would have to be viewed in two phases: BC and AD. These men would find themselves in a garden with the Son of God doing what He does best, comforting the brokenhearted, healing, and restoring. It's like déjà vu. "Jesus Christ, the same yesterday, today and forever" (Heb. 13:8).

Jesus's whole ministry, from Eden to Gethsemane to the cross, was all about humankind. Compassion for our condition ruled the day. We were captives to sin and all its horrible effects, and we are helpless pawns in the hand of the enemy of our soul. Without God on our side, we were doomed to failure, defeat, and eternal death—never to be reunited with the God of love and mercy and forever to be buffeted by a savage, barbaric master. God would not have been unjust had He allowed us to reap what we sowed. But the Bible tells us that He loved us with an everlasting love and with loving-kindness He has drawn us (Jer. 31:3).

Jesus put it all on the line to come to our rescue even though it was clear that humankind was not willing to receive Him, accept Him, or yield to Him. Man did not know how feeble and futile self-effort is against "the wiles of the devil." We are so aghast at man's inhumanity to man. Sometimes we are horrified at man's defiance of the sovereignty and majesty of God. We are always amazed at the long-suffering of God. He remembers "our frame; He remembers that we are dust" (Ps. 103:14).

As extraordinary as humankind is—glowing achievements in every field and area of study and stunning accomplishments in science, athletics, and the arts across the cultural spectrum—many innovations are to be proud of and even be very grateful for. But as the applause grows louder, the arrogance grows exponentially. And so, now man is deceived into believing the lie that started in the garden of Eden, "Hath God said? For God doth know that in the day ye eat thereof, then your eyes shall be opened, and ye shall be as God, knowing good and evil" (Gen.3:5). Inference is that then man will not need God if man will be as God.

If only we could perhaps skywrite it in a language understood by all that God alone is God and man is only mere man. Only the empowerment of God Himself makes man the model of genius, exploits, and adventurism that he is. If only man gave the glory where it is due. If only he recognized that it all comes from God and is distributed severally as He chooses and can be withdrawn at His will. **If** only man's motives were not corrupt and selfish. What God could accomplish through man that is completely yielded to His will and His glory! **And so He issues the call.**

The call is urgent from the heart of God, "not willing that any should perish" (2 Pet. 3:9). It is a plain and simple call, "Come." It matters not that you do not know or understand the terms of the contract, the covenant. All that matters is that you come. "Just as you are," He says. Deign to take Him up on His offer and His promises. He is willing to discuss it with you and walk you through all of it. He was willing to send His only begotten Son to die on your behalf while you were still nonchalant and heedless. All those bursts of conscience that have been in your path, compelling you to do the right thing, was, in fact, the God of Creation talking to you, wanting to engage with you. God wants to lovingly have a discourse with you before time runs out. Because when eternity is ushered in, it will be too late. Everyone's fate will be sealed, whatever your choice.

God gave us His Word—His written Word—to which He held not only man but also Himself accountable. God gave us the bond of His Holy Spirit to carry out His will and to seal them who are His. God gave us His Son, the final solution, the written Word made flesh and dwelt amongst us, the living Word. It was all He could do. God can do no more to affect our salvation. The transaction is complete. The covenant is sealed in the blood of Jesus. It is an unbreakable covenant. It awaits your signature, your acceptance of the Lord Jesus Christ.

So He continues to call, to warn of impending doom and to offer safe haven. Come. Jesus issued a call at the outset of His ministry for a standard of excellence, a life of selfless service and above reproach. In His Sermon on the Mount, He laid out the lifestyle He came to offer us. We are called to deny self. We are called to extraordinary service and concern for others, truly no one left behind. We are called to a moral high ground, worthy of the name of the Lord and of the faith for which we are exhorted to contend. Jesus turned the rules, regulations, and protocols of man on its head. He challenged us instead to be "perfect, even as your Father who is in heaven is perfect."

It's a tall order indeed, but He made the way for us. Now He calls us to believe, to accept, and to receive. There is no other way. There aren't several options. Sin will yield to no other master. Satan will bow to no other Lord. God will accept no less a price than the perfect, sinless Lamb to pardon our sins. Only Jesus can satisfy the demand. The apostle Peter laid it out clearly and plainly as he addressed the rulers, elders, and scribes after the day of Pentecost. Acts 4:12 reads, "Neither is there salvation in any other; for there is no other name under heaven given among men, whereby we must be saved."

The apostle Paul reiterated this very revelation in his letter to the Philippians. Philippians 2:9–11 says, "Wherefore, God hath also highly exalted Him, and given Him a name which is above every name; that at the name of Jesus every knee shall bow, of things in heaven, and things in earth, and things under earth; and that every tongue should confess that Jesus Christ is Lord, to the glory of God, the Father."

All the writings of the New Testament—the new covenant—makes Jesus Christ the center of gravity of earth's activity, its future, and its final outcome. Revelation 4:11 says, "Thou art worthy O Lord, to receive glory and power; for thou hast created all things, and for thy pleasure they are and were created."

That's the new status quo of the "new heaven and the

new earth." The Lamb of God who takes away the sin of the world (John 1:29) is in charge here. All of creation is subject to Him. Revelation 21:27 reads, "And there shall in no way enter into it anything that defileth, he that worketh abomination, or maketh a lie, but they who are written in the Lamb's Book of Life.

Creation is transformed and made new through the shed blood of Jesus. It all pivots around Jesus. The lowly carpenter's son, "despised and rejected of men," is exalted. This is fullness of joy. But while there is still time and mercy in abundance, Jesus calls us relentlessly to come. The urgency is so downright alarming that the complacency that abounds is disturbing. Every detail has been taken care of by Father, Son, and Holy Ghost in order to pay the price of redemption for all humankind. Yet many turn their backs, and others give little more than lip service.

Matthew 15:8 says, "This people draweth near unto me with their mouth and honoreth with their lips, but their heart is far from me." And John 5:40 reads, "And ye will not come to me, that ye might have life."

In the life of the believer, Jesus should be the center of gravity. Thus He sorely wants to be to the nonbeliever. As children of God, we are the witnesses to the lost and dying world that Jesus truly makes the difference in our life and any life yielded to Him. The blessings we receive of His bounty must be showcased in our daily lives, clear for anyone to see. We do the Lord a grave disservice when our lives send mixed signals and when we have a double standard, one for ourselves and another for everyone else. No doubt we confuse the onlookers when we are not consistent and utterly dependable.

As with our Father, our word must be our bond. Our hearts must be ready to reach out to the needy, our hands must be ready to labor in love, and our feet must be ready to bring good news of God's love, grace, and justice for all. Micah 6:8 says, "He hath shown thee O man, what is good; and what doth the Lord require of thee, but to do justly, to love mercy, and to walk humbly with thy God."

This was the intent from the beginning, before that terrible day with its tragic fallout. The devastation sin wreaks in life, home, and community in every nation, creed, and race—all of creation—is unquestionably horrible. The enemy of humankind and God alike is determined to steal, kill, and destroy as ruinously as he can in the time allotted him. The lure of fame and fortune charm so many, but they fail to discern the shadowy figure lurking in the background. They delude themselves that they're charting their own course, that is, "doing their own thing," and therefore do not need God or His ways to make it in this life. All the while, sin takes its daily deadly toll, and lives are cheated out of an eternity of bliss with God. "What shall it profit a man if he shall gain the whole world and lose his own soul?" (Mark 8:36).

This is a beautiful world indeed in which we live. On a clear day, the vastness of the blue sky with its billowy white clouds is breathtaking. Seen from an airplane, it is such a moving sight. On a dark night, away from the glaring city lights, the multitude of stars comes out of hiding, and what a brilliant entrance they make! How vast is the ocean! The seas, rivers, lakes, streams, brooks, and springs all began in the mind of God, along with towering mountains, giant trees, landscapes of rock, flowers of varied hues and forms, and soil rich in color and goodness. Verdant, lush foliage and vines that explore far and wide. Boundless savannahs and forests support exotic creatures and life-forms of every description. Natural wonders boggle our minds and keep us wondering. Mysteries that challenge the intellect open the way for new and remarkable discoveries. Technology is continually transforming our world and pushing the boundaries of outer space and the ocean depths.

It is a wonderful world. And God made it so. But the taint of sin runs through it. Its true beauty is tarnished. God has promised that He will make a new heaven and a new earth free of sin, forever unblemished, forever lovely, forever to be under the direct governance of God.

Revelation 21:1–2 says, "And I saw a new heaven and a new earth; for the first heaven and the first earth passed away, and there was no more sea … the holy city, new Jerusalem, coming down from God out of heaven prepared as a bride adorned for her husband." And Revelation 21:24–25 reads, "And the nations of them who are saved shall walk in the light of it, and the kings of the earth do bring their glory and honor into it. And the gates of it shall not be shut at all by day; for there shall be no night there."

It's an endless day in an endless world of indescribable beauty to dwell in, to explore, and to enjoy endlessly in the presence of the King of Kings and Lord of Lords. We will all cast our crowns before Him for eternity! The promise of eternal life is an enduring beacon of hope down through the ages. Jesus taught us not to hold on to this life at the expense of life everlasting in glory.

There is much in this life to challenge us and to especially defy our faith in God and His covenant promises.

Jesus forewarned us that we would suffer persecutions and have tribulations. As much as it will not be smooth sailing all of the time, His grace abundant will suffice to keep us safe in His arms for eternity, no matter the outcome of our tribulations in this life. His promise never to leave us nor forsake us buoys our courage to press on in the face of disappointment, discouragement, and distress. The way from earth to heaven—from eternal death to eternal life— leads through the cross. Humankind is deceived into thinking that there are many ways to heaven: religions, philosophies, and ideologies, all man-made. There is the price that Jesus had to pay and the fact He struggled within Himself whether there was some other way, "O my Father, if it be possible, let this cup pass from me; nevertheless, not as I will but as thou wilt" (Matt.26:39).

This tells us in no uncertain terms that there was no other way. There is no other way to heaven, save through the blood-drenched cross and the tremendous price it exacted. What could be substituted? What could equate? How could our mind even attempt to conceive its equal? Such a thought has only one origin, Satan. There is no other way except the way of the cross. "Nothing but the blood of Jesus." That blood of the new and everlasting covenant secures for us a place out of this sin-weary world. It grants us citizenship in the very kingdom of the Highest God. We become His subjects; He is our reigning king. Under the terms of the covenant, He sees to our welfare, "Hath given unto us all things that pertain to life and godliness" (2 Pet. 1:3). The vast majority of us have no line of communication with the powers-that-be in this world. But we are personally linked to the Absolute Power over all. We enjoy access to the King of Kings, direct access, that is. So amazing! There's no chain of command to navigate. Just a broken and contrite heart.

Not only does God welcome us, He insists that we come. He is grieved that too many do not. The scars that Jesus bears roars ever louder above the shouts and clamoring of a world that is distorted in its thinking. That puts a stamp of approval on what is wrong and then persecutes and prosecutes what is the right. The cross is steadily shoved to the background and out of view when it should rightfully dominate the foreground. The new life in Christ is looked on with disdain and revulsion. The lifestyle of debauchery and lewdness is lauded and desired. The Christ of the passion is deemed a folklore, of no real relevance to forward-thinking people of scholarship and renown. A new day is on the horizon though. Daily life as we know it will suddenly come to a screeching halt.

Matthew 24:30 says, "And then shall appear the sign of the Son of Man in heaven; and then shall all the tribes of the earth mourn, and they shall see the Son of Man coming in the clouds of heaven with power and great glory." And John 5:28 states, "Marvel not at this; for the hour is coming, in which all that are in the grave shall hear his His voice." The invitation to "come" is still open and inclusive, and all are welcome. Reserve your place!

Isaiah 1:18 reads, "Come now and let us reason together, saith the Lord; though your sins be as scarlet, they shall be as white as snow; though they be red like crimson they shall be as wool." And Isaiah 55:1 says, "Ho everyone that thirsteth, come to the waters, and he that hath no money;

come, buy and eat; yea come buy wine and milk without money and without price."

Salvation is full and free; life is eternal with the Lord of Glory. The offer does not expire until we do, if we fail to accept it.

CHAPTER 4

SEARCH AND RESCUE

MATTHEW 28:19 SAYS, "Go ye therefore into all the world." Jesus's Great Commission is the launchpad for multiple outreaches all over the globe. Missionary efforts bring relief to a variety of needs in impoverished communities the world over. Portals of entry for ministering the gospel of Jesus Christ swing open as a result of many faith-based programs that address physical and social needs. As Jesus went about doing good, He left us an example. More than that, He firmly exhorts us in His Word to reach out to those in need. Too often, the poor are overlooked and largely voiceless, or their cries fall on deaf ears. The Lord Jesus Christ calls us to "go into all the world." Wherever there are needs, the collective body, the church, is usually front and center. We must go to the needy wherever they are. Sometimes they are isolated in some of the remotest parts of the world. Other times, social behavior—or rather misbehavior—creates the field of missions. Then there is the plight of the homeless. There are orphans and parent-deprived children everywhere needing open arms and hearts to open warm, loving, stable homes to receive them. Jesus's ministry never sidestepped the poor, the disaffected, and the disadvantaged. In fact, Jesus identified with these. Coming down from heaven, God incarnate chose to be born among the poor rather than in a palace. He lived and grew up on the so-called wrong side of the tracks. When He launched His ministry, the question was asked, "Can any good thing come out of Nazareth?"

The world is full of desperate people trying to survive meagerly one day at a time. Children are desperately hungry and malnourished. Sitting at death's door, they are brought within our range of vision via the media and they leave an indelible image upon our conscience. As victims of war, disasters, crimes, and injustices, they cry out in despair. There are just so many dark places where the enemy hides out and perpetrates his grisly deeds that forever scars the lives of too many of our youngsters—from the affluent to the poor, at home and abroad. The grinding poverty, spiritual and material, breeds the hopelessness and despair that abounds in many hearts.

As it is viewed from our humble perch and our limited perspective, the task is so very daunting. But we are backed by heaven's resources. His blood-bought covenant promises are made accessible to His church, promises that are secured in the new and everlasting covenant in His blood, promises that He commissions us to go and proclaim to the destitute and utterly hopeless, "strangers from the covenants of promise, having no hope and without God in the world" (Eph. 2:12). He wants them to hear how He took their pain and sorrow to the cross and how He purchased "a new and living way" for them. His heart breaks to see so many pressing on with such meager fare amidst a world so affluent. His is a worldview like no other.

Many stories have been told, and several books have been written about the lives of men and women who have been touched by God and moved by His Spirit to carry His love, grace, and blessings to the farthest corners of the world, always searching out the poor and needy and coming to their rescue. Untold numbers have been reached and touched with His presence—and His presents—bringing new life to them.

And the Work Goes On

'Til the end of time, our Lord will be calling up His troops and deploying them near and far to proclaim the good news of the gospel. The campaign is ongoing for souls for the kingdom of God. To borrow a line from the book *The Hiding Place*, "There is no pit so deep that He is not deeper still." God can transcend every barrier, every wall, and every prison—and He does—to reach, rescue, and redeem His lost children. His heart grieves for their plight. His heart must cheer for those who heed His call, surrender all, and go at His bidding. He sends out His search party to rescue the perishing wherever they may be. They—and we—are all His. He never gives us up without a fight, and He never loses a battle unless we give up.

The needs that plague so many disaffected people everywhere have become more complex and direr as the years roll on. The message of faith in Jesus Christ is more urgent than ever and is reaching into every country and walk of life, bringing hope through the preaching of the gospel; the meeting of those urgent needs of healing and health, food, clothing, and shelter; and giving precious people created and loved by God a fresh start to help change their circumstances.

Jesus emphatically expounded in His Word about this responsibility that we have to extend His love to those less fortunate. God is never oblivious to their plight, contrary to some lines of thinking. We are His agents to deliver His goodwill and to proclaim His goodness to all humankind. When He comes in glory and gathers all nations before Him, this will be a priority.

It stands to reason that this is a priority we do well to give allegiance to. It is commendable that we give and especially that many give generously to numerous missions and charitable foundations. The question is, "Are we doing all we can?" We need the wisdom of God to lead us in view of the magnitude of the problems and the difficulty to wade through the tangled web that presents as urgent humanitarian needs. But the admonition is clear, search for and rescue the perishing. We ignore it at our own peril.

The challenge is to deny the kingdom of darkness the souls for whom Christ died and made provisions for, under the covenant in His blood. The challenge is to reach them and tell them in order to win them for Christ. Many of God's people are on the firing lines, doing the heavy lifting to bring light into the darkness. Many have left their mark on the landscape of the mission field; some have lost their lives in the line of duty. God honors their sacred work in His Word, and it is our legacy to perpetuate.

How Incredibly Christ like.

Matthew 25:35–40 says,

> I was hungry and you gave me food, I was thirsty and ye gave me drink; I was a stranger and ye took me in; naked and ye clothe me; sick and ye visited me; I was in prison and ye came unto me. Then shall the righteous answer Him saying, Lord, when saw we thee hungry and fed thee; or thirsty and gave thee drink? When saw we thee a stranger and took thee in; or naked and clothed thee? Or when saw we thee sick, or in prison, and came unto thee? And the King shall answer and say unto them, verily I say unto you inasmuch as ye have done it unto one of the least of these my brethren, ye have done it unto me.

Nehemiah 8:10 states, "Go your way, eat the fat, and drink the sweet, and send portions unto them for whom nothing is prepared ... for the joy of the Lord is your strength."

Anywhere people are deprived of the basics that provide for simple human dignity and basic freedom and justice, God sends His presence and bestows His grace in the persons of those whose hearts and lives have been touched and transformed by His incomparable love. Only our Lord living on the inside of a man and the power of His Word and the Holy Spirit can produce the pure, selfless dedication to service that stands in defiance of the negligence and indifference of the powers-that-be. The scope of the problems is oftentimes beyond the reach of just the auspices of the church, and groups focused on humanitarian issues find the church a worthy partner. God's model is pure and simple, "Freely ye have received, freely give" (Matt. 10:8).

CHAPTER 5

AN ENDURING LEGACY

A s WE HURTLE TO the final countdown to that Last Day, the call from our Lord to "come" and "go" becomes more urgent by the day. The race is heating up. The devil knows his time is shorter than it was before, and he is stepping up his game with deadly consequences. We hear and see the carnage and wreckage everywhere. There is no mercy or compassion. There's only blind ideologies and blind leaders of the blind. There is fear all around. The very things that are a boon are turned into a nightmarish curse unleashed in terror against humanity. Brain and brawn are diverted from noble humanitarian aspirations and is channeled into the most horrific endeavors.

Man cannot be trusted to uphold the good of humanity of his own volition. Apart from Christ, man cannot be entrusted with the life of the planet. The creation that God lovingly brought into being and supremely sacrificed to redeem cannot be left to the whims of arrogant humans who deny the very existence of God, propagate man-made theories, and deem themselves to be the ultimate authority, accountable to none higher. Ludicrous!

Good news! God will take the reins. "… to them that look for Him shall He appear" (Heb. 9:28). In the meantime, amidst the times of conflicts on every hand, distress of nations, and mounting uncertainties, the children of God—the church—marches on. Against all odds and in the face of ever-increasing adversities, the church thrives, lives, and gives new life to the perishing, the bread of life to the hungry, and the water springing up into everlasting life to the thirsty. The church is so often the last bastion of hope for souls that have been failed by everything the world offered. When the deception of the enemy is unveiled and sin is revealed for what it is, the church is on the front lines of the battle. The church is down in the trenches with the downtrodden. Wherever there is a cry for help from God Almighty, there is the church.

God works through His church, through His elect, to bring His love and grace to those who do not know and have not heard, to bring His light to the ones that sit in immense darkness, and to give a hand of rescue to souls perilously close to the brink of eternal damnation. He still seeks and saves to the uttermost anyone who will receive Him. He still makes Himself known to every creature "that men may know" (Ps. 83:18). He is not willing that any should perish. The invitation is extended. You are welcome.

Revelation 22:17 says, "And the Spirit and the Bride say come. And let him that heareth say come. And let him that is athirst come. And whosoever will, let him take the water of life freely." He has made everything ready for you. You are to be the guest of honor. Make haste and come. Jesus will see you now!

As Jesus was contemplating the end time with His disciples, He spoke a parable in which He said, "Occupy till I come." Many years have come and gone since then. And many signs of His second coming have appeared on the horizon. One thing is absolutely certain: we are closer now than when we first believed.

There is still much to be done, and we cannot grow weary in doing well. It takes strong commitment and resolve and much sacrifice to do the work of the ministry and carry forward the mandate of the church. But so many lives depend on what we do. We cannot afford to drop the ball. It is Christ first in all we do. It must be so if we call Him Lord. Our love for our Savior leads us into service; His love for us drives all our efforts. His heart beats within us and pumps out compassion and mercy for the poor and needy, for the lost and dying. As God blesses our lives with His abundance, we are charged to be good stewards of the resources He entrusts to us. Our service is valued by Him and encouraged in the Word of God. In fact, He equates laboring on behalf of those in need with giving unto Him. As children of His love, what we do in His name must be wrapped in His love. We do not get to choose whom we should show His love to or whom we serve. Our "neighbor" may very well be that "Samaritan" that embodies all our prejudices. It is our God-ordained duty to help our Samaritans to the best of our ability with a generous helping of the love of God. It is God's duty to transform them.

We are His servants, poised to do His bidding. However, unless we declutter our minds by praying the mind that was in Christ Jesus would also be in us, we run the risk of having God's directions to us get lost in all our clutter: our own thoughts and ideas; our own personal prejudices; our pride; and our grand opinion of our self. As we humble ourselves under the mighty hand of God, we are better able to see others through the prism that God sees them because our self is cut down to size. Jesus is our model. If anyone should be demanding or deprecating, it is our Lord. Yet He humbled Himself "unto death; even the death on the cross"—as humiliating as it was. He lowered Himself into the very dust to reach out to a soul in need of His grace and mercy—a woman caught in adultery. Even now, exalted in heaven, seated at the right hand of God the Father, He is "touched with the feelings of our infirmities" (Heb. 4:15).

He looks beyond our faults and sees our need, the songwriter said. The world is full of walking faults and needs, and we are His hands extended. He never discriminates. Neither can we. "Ours is not to question why; ours is but to do and die." This must be our mind-set in the service of the King of Kings. Wherever He places us, His love must shine forth. That is our mandate. We engage with our fellow man. We adapt and be relevant. We preach the Word. We occupy 'til He comes.

We Are the Church!

We are set apart to stand out from the rest. God is in the midst of us, guiding and directing His work. Miracles are wrought by His power so there is no denying that our God is mighty. We know He lives because He lives in us. That sets the church of Jesus Christ apart from the rest. In the parable of the laborers (Matt. 20:10), all received the same wages regardless of time spent in the field. There was no graded scale there. There was no upper and lower class. There was no room for pride and arrogance. What God desires for one, He prepares for all. None is excluded from partaking of the inheritance bequeathed to us by the blood of the new and everlasting covenant. To be deceived again into giving up our estate will be beyond tragic. It would be completely foolish. Job 33:14 states, "For God speaketh once, yea twice, yet man perceiveth not."

God desires so much better for us. It is truly tragic that man would rather settle for Satan's counterfeit than receive God's genuine best. God gives us the lasting presence of the Holy Spirit within to daily lead the child of God as we wind our way from time to eternity. The journey between those two points is fraught with contradictions: highs and lows; joys and sorrows; and accomplishments and disappointments. The sum total of our experiences incorporates all the variations of life on earth, some of which are too overwhelming to overcome without the help and grace of God. Particularly in those times, we learn the true value of the treasure we have in our earthen vessel, Christ in us and the indwelling Holy Spirit. We learn the power of the Word of God that will not pass away. We come to value the gift of God Himself in our life. He comes into our life loaded with other gifts to make us valuable citizens of earth but, more importantly, to make our life's journey victorious over the carefully crafted traps and snares of the devil to derail us and totally deprive us of our expected end.

Our lives are blessed with the virtues that exemplify

the character of God, our Father. We are enabled to take a stand for righteousness, morality, and plain old common decency and integrity. We desire to live right for the gospel's sake that we may be worthy witnesses of our Lord and Savior Jesus Christ. We are made righteous through His precious blood, and His presence within us is able to transform us into honest and trustworthy human beings. Our selfish ways must give place to generous hearts that God can use to bless others. The peace is beyond all human understanding. The fruit of the Spirit defies our carnal, self-centered yearnings. Faith and hope—our virtual twin towers—drive us ever onward and upward in our thinking and actions.

These are eternal gifts bestowed upon our mortal bodies to create a people of the Lord. And God has promised in His Word that, if we would make the things of His kingdom our first priority, the material blessings that are necessary to life on Planet Earth will not be denied us. The chasing after things that are temporal and of little or no spiritual significance is deadly to our soul and our bodies as well. We have God's Word that He will take care of us during our sojourn here on earth and He will equip us for our transition to our eternal inheritance. We have a blood covenant with the eternal God! There is no comparison with the legacy of the world.

Thousands of years of Satan's dominance in the mind of the unbelievers have not yielded a people of exemplary character. Lives have been led down a path that leads to destruction and devastation. The ones who refuse God's outstretched arm do not notice the subtle approach of the enemy. It is a well-laid plan to snare as many as he can to deny them the heritage that he lost and can never regain. How sad it would be, if you had this moment, this opportunity to "taste and see that the Lord is good" (Ps. 34:8) and then to miss it, only to find out much too late that you were wrong and God was right.

This is the time to seriously think about eternity and where we are going to spend it, eternal life or eternal death. The choice is ours to make, but God gives us His best advice. He urges us to choose life. It is folly to spurn His advice or downplay His warning. The cost was too high; the stakes are too enormous. You are too precious. A call from a heart seeking His mercy is never put on hold. He is waiting. Don't fall for the same old deception. Acts 16:31 says, "Believe on the Lord Jesus Christ and thou shalt be saved and thy house."

Be set apart for a glorious eternity. Be a bona fide member of the body, the church of the Lord Jesus Christ. She is His bride! Revelation 19:7 says, "Let us be glad and rejoice and give Him glory, for the marriage of the Lamb has come, and His wife has made herself ready."

The truth is that He made His wife ready. He laid down His life for His church. He purchased us with His blood, the blood of the new and everlasting covenant, that covenant from which He never retreats. The blood of Jesus washes and cleanses us from all sin and makes us ready for our heavenly bridal attire, "arrayed in fine linen, clean and white; for the fine linen is the righteousness of saints" (Rev. 19:8). We are clothed in the "garments of salvation" and the "robe of righteousness," all provided through the shed blood of our Lord and Savior Jesus Christ.

When time shall be no more, the dawn of the new day

breaks forth, and the church is free of any spot or wrinkle, adorned to meet the bridegroom, we will be ushered into the marriage supper. As the closing act plays out on the earth, the children of God enter into their rest. All the trials and the tribulations are over. All of the world's glitz and glamour fade in the face of heaven's unrivaled, untainted beauty. All tears are dried. Every voice is finely tuned and in perfect harmony, lifted with unbridled joy in praise to the King of Kings and Lord of Lords! A congregation of saints gathers of every tribe, nation, and language. All are God's children; all are brethren. Father, Son, and Holy Ghost are at the controls.

It is eternity, and it will never end!

EPILOGUE

GOD IS NOT SEEKING our demise or destruction. His all-out effort is to deliver us from evil and to translate us into His kingdom. All powerful, He has the power to accomplish this, but it is left to us to make the choice to serve Him or not. Love is costly. Loving us cost Him dearly, but He willingly paid the price to redeem us to Himself. He presents us with a package of benefits purchased with the blood of His only begotten Son, Jesus Christ. His love for us inspires us to love, first Him—Father, Son, and Holy Ghost—and then others.

Real love will cost us too. It cannot be in word only, but in word and in deed. God demonstrated His love toward us. We ought to demonstrate our love toward others by actions that say we love. He is building a family of blood-washed saints who are not afraid to be radically transformed until we look radically different from the world. He is calling together a body that, but for the love of God, would be incohesive and fractious. This army of believers propagates the kingdom message to defeat the gross darkness in the earth and in men's soul. This message of salvation liberates the captives and brings the good news that we have new life in Christ here and an eternal heritage hereafter. We lost it all in the garden. He regained it all for us at the cross.

As the enemy steps up his efforts to push his agenda—steal, kill, and destroy—and as he does it with increasing gore—his counterfeit sacrifice—God counteracts with increasing throngs being delivered from the cruel grip of that gross darkness which the devil has inflicted on the unsuspecting soul and from empty religious ideologies that he has used from time immemorial to enslave the mind of man. But God's Word breaks through.

We, his blood-bought church, must stay true and committed to God's agenda. We must stand our ground in the name of the Lord and keep the message in the air and His loving kindness front and center. A deceived world is blindly headed to its final doomsday. Lives are at stake, lives for which Christ died. Jesus is the only antidote to the virulence of the attacks from the enemy of our soul so he could deter us from salvation and eternal life that God has prepared for those that love Him, blood covenant promises.

As we go and give and share His love, others will hear of the great God who gave it all for His lost and broken children. And they will come to know Him and go and tell others that the Lamb was slain and we are redeemed! And then shall the end come.

How very gracious. Hallelujah!

BIBLIOGRAPHY

Blood Covenant

Google/the Covenant Kingdom
www.the-covenant-kingdom.com: Online teaching by Rob
    Board
Google/Got Questions? Org: Online
Merriam-Webster Pocket Dictionary

Scourge

Merriam-Webster Pocket Dictionary

Crucifixion

Merriam-Webster Pocket Dictionary

Quotes

The Hiding Place by Corrie Ten Boom: "There is no pit so
    deep, that He is not deeper still."
"The Charge of the Light Brigade" by Alfred Lord Tennyson:
    "Ours is not to question why; ours is but to do and die."

"Master the tempest is raging," Hymn #102, *Favorite Hymns of Praise*

"Nothing but the Blood," Hymn #138, *Favorite Hymns of Praise*

"From every stormy wind," Hymn #1171, *Sankey's Sacred Songs and Solos*

"The Love of God," Hymn #166, *Favorite Hymns of Praise*

Scriptures

All scripture references taken from *The New Scofield Study Bible KJV*, previously published as *The New Scofield Reference Bible*

Scripture References

Old Testament

Genesis 1:1, 27 ; 2:1, 3; 3:5, 15, 22; 9:9, 13–16; 17:1

Exodus 4:26

Nehemiah 8:10

Numbers 23:19

1 Chron. 29:11

Job 33:14; 34:21; 36:27, 28; 37:3; 38:8-11; 39:1, 9, 27; 41:1, 3, 4

Psalm 34:8; 68:19; 103:14; 104:27, 28; 119:89; 124:7; 139:7–10; 138:2

Proverbs 15:3

Isaiah 1:18; 11:2; 40:14; 41:21–23, 24, 28; 43:26; 44:6; 45:12, 18, 22; 52:14; 53:6, 12; 55:1

Jeremiah 29:11; 31:3; 32:27

Daniel 2:21; 5:21

New Testament

Matthew 8:26–27; 11:28–30; 13:24-25; 14:33; 15:8; 16:16, 18; 24:14, 30; 25:35-40; 26:39; 27:29, 30

Mark 8:36; 16:15

Luke 7:39-40; 10:19; 13:16

John 2:24, 25; 3:16; 5:28; 14:1-30; 15:13; 19:1, 17–18

Acts 1:8; 4:12; 16:31; 17:24, 25

Romans 8:18

1 Corinthians 2:7–8

Galatians 3:14

Ephesians 1:13–14; 2:8–9, 12; 3:9, 11

Philippians 2:9–11

2 Timothy 2:15; 4:7

Hebrews 4:15; 9:14; 10:19–20, 39; 11:6; 13:5, 8

James 1:14

1 Peter 1:18, 19

2 Peter 3:9

1 John 2:10, 3:16; 4:10

Jude 20

Revelation 2:10; 4:11; 19:7, 8 ; 21:1–2, 24–25, 27; 22:12, 17

Printed in the United States
By Bookmasters